MACHYNLLETH TO BARMOUTH

Vic Mitchell and Keith Smith

MP Middleton Press

Front cover: Approaching Tywyn on 24th June 1981 is no. M56155 working the 15.18 Machynlleth to Barmouth. The Wharf station of the Talyllyn Railway is behind the class 103 DMU. (T.Heavyside)

Back cover: To universal surprise, steam returned to the route and 4-6-0 no. 7506 was photographed running south from Barmouth on 28th May 1987. The headboard proclaims "Cardigan Bay Express", but the train ran only between Barmouth and Machynlleth. (B.Robbins)

Published August 2009

ISBN 978 1 906008 54 3

© *Middleton Press, 2009*

Design Deborah Esher
Typesetting Barbara Mitchell

Published by
 Middleton Press
 Easebourne Lane
 Midhurst
 West Sussex
 GU29 9AZ
Tel: 01730 813169
Fax: 01730 812601
Email: info@middletonpress.co.uk
www.middletonpress.co.uk

Printed in the United Kingdom by Henry Ling Limited, at the Dorset Press, Dorchester, DT1 1HD

INDEX

ACKNOWLEDGEMENTS

We are very grateful for the assistance received from many of those mentioned in the credits also to P.G.Barnes, J.L.H.Bate, W.R.Burton, A.R.Carder, L.Crosier, G.Croughton, F.Hornby, C.Jepson, N.Langridge, B.Lewis, C.G.Maggs, A.Rhodes, D.T.Rowe, Mr D. and Dr S.Salter, G.Williams and in particular, our always supportive wives, Barbara Mitchell and Janet Smith.

I. Railway Clearing House map for 1904.

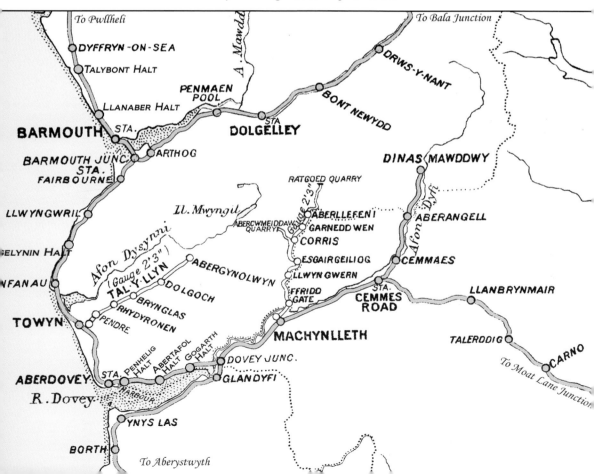

GEOGRAPHICAL SETTING

The Cambrian Mountains are cut through on their western flank by two major rivers, the Dovey and the Mawddach. Our route follows the former from Machynlleth to the coast and crosses it at Dovey Junction. The Mawddach is crossed at its mouth, on the approach to Barmouth, by means of the well known wooden bridge, shown later.

Most of the rocks traversed are ancient deposits and there are some lava extrusions near the line north of Tywyn. Between there and Llwyngwril is a triangle of land separated from the rest of Wales by a major fault. The Bala Fault runs northeast. That part of the route south of the River Dovey was built in Montgomeryshire and the section north of it was laid in Merionethshire.

Welsh spelling and hyphenation has varied over the years and so we have generally used the most recent form as have the railways. The maps are to the scale of 25ins to 1 mile, with north at the top, unless otherwise indicated.

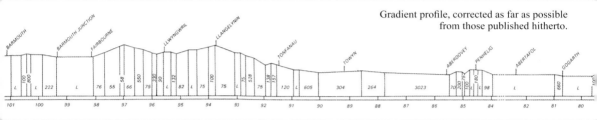

Gradient profile, corrected as far as possible from those published hitherto.

HISTORICAL BACKGROUND

The Newtown & Machynlleth Railway was authorised in 1857 and opened west to Borth on 1st July 1863. Completion to Aberystwyth was undertaken by the Aberystwyth & Welsh Coast Railway on 23rd June 1864 and all these lines became part of the new Cambrian Railways in 1864-65.

The A&WCR extended northwards by opening the Aberdovey to Llwyngwril section on 24th October 1863. The CR finished the route in stages. Llwyngwril north to Penmaenpool (two miles west of Dolgelley) followed on 3rd July 1865 and it was extended to that town in 1868, where it made a connection with the new Bala & Dolgelley Railway.

Barmouth Junction (Morfa Mawddach from 1960) to Pwllheli opened on 3rd June 1867 and Dovey Junction (Glandovey Junction until 1904) to Aberdovey followed on 14th August of that year. The railway ferry service from the Aberystwyth line then ceased. The Cambrian Railways became part of the Great Western Railway in 1922.

With the advent of nationalisation, all lines in the area became part of the Western Region of British Railways on 1st January 1948. The route was transferred to the London Midland Region on 17th June 1963.

Closure of the route was threatened and the Cambrian Coast Line Action Group was formed in 1971. It was extremely active and victory was achieved in July 1974. However, in April 1980, Barmouth Bridge was declared unsafe, but further campaigning resulted in repairs during a brief closure period and its reopening in May 1981. The group organised Sunday trains that Summer. Subsequently most level crossings were automated as an economy measure.

An important event in the history of the line took place in October 1988, when a Radio Electronic Token Block system was introduced, the control being at Machynlleth.

Privatisation resulted in Central Trains operating services from 2nd March 1997. However, after reorganisation in October 2001, Wales & Borders became the franchisee. Arriva Trains Wales took over in December 2003.

The European Rail Traffic Management System was introduced in experimental form in 2008, prior to its use on the Thameslink route in Central London.

PASSENGER SERVICES

The figures quoted are for weekday trains. One train ran on Sundays in most years, but often for only two or three months in the Summer.

For most of the 1860s, there were three trains and for many years the destination of most was Dolgelley and not Barmouth, including the Sunday mail train. In the early months, the connection across Barmouth Bridge was horsedrawn.

The frequency had increased to six a day by 1905, but was back to three by 1925. It was 5 in 1940, 7 in 1955, 6 in 1971, 8 in 1985 and 10 in 2008. The few short workings are not included.

Through trains (or coaches) from London were known as the "Cambrian Coast Express" from 1927 and ran from Paddington until 1967, war years excepted. The London terminus then became Euston, although the train name was not used again until 1986. The service was Summer only and later restricted to Saturdays only. The name was changed to the "Snowdonian".

August 1893

WHITCHURCH, OSWESTRY, ABERYSTWYTH, BARMOUTH, PWLLHELI, &c.—Cambrian.
Offices—Oswestry.   Sec. and Gen. Man., Alfred Aslett.   Asst. Sec., R. Brayne.

September 1925

MACHYNLLETH, BARMOUTH, and PWLLHELI.—Great Western (late Cambrian).

Miles	Down. Week Days.	mrn	mrn	mrn	mrn	mrn	mrn	mrn	mrn	mrn	Through Carriages, Portmadoc and Criccieth to Manchester (Exchange) and Liverpool (Lime St.) see pages 407 & 397.	aft	mrn	mrn	aft	aft
	Machynlleth ....dep.				6 10			8 20					10 53			
3¾	Dovey Junction ....arr.							8 27					11 0			
—	138 Aberystwyth ..dep.							7 50					10 20			
—	Dovey Junction ¶ ..dep.							8 38					11 10			
9¾	Aberdovey				6 30			8 53					11 24			
13½	Towyn A 946				6 38			9 1					11 32			
15¾	Tonfanau				Aa			9 6					11 37			
20	Llwyngwril				6 50			9 14					11 46			
22¾	Fairbourne, for Friog				6 59			9 23					11 55			
23¾	Barmouth Junc. 145 arr.				7 2			9 25					11 58			
33	Dolgelley 144, 145 arr.				8 5			10n3		m			12n56			m
	Dolgelley 144, 145 dep.					7 0		8n50	9 45	1040				1145		1 35
—	Barmouth Junction.dep.				7 3	7 20		9 27	1011	1059			12 0	12 6		1 55
25½	Barmouth ¶ arr.				7 8	7 25		9 32	1016	11 4			12 5	1211		2 0
	Barmouth ¶ dep.					7 40		9 37		11 5					1220	2 15
30½	Dyffryn-on-Sea ¶					7 50		9 47		1118					1230	2 28
33½	Llanbedr and Pensarn					7 57		9 54		1125					1237	2 35
36	Harlech					8 6		10 2							1246	
39½	Talsarnau					8 14		10 11							1253	
41½	Penrhyndeudraeth					8 19		10 16							1258	
42½	Minffordd 949					8 24		10 21							1 3	
44¾	Portmadoc B ¶ arr.					8 28		10 25							1 10	
	Portmadoc B ¶ dep.		6 40			8 40	9 25	10 29				12 40			1 20	
49¾	Criccieth		6 50			8 51	9 35	10 40				12 51			1 30	
53	Afon Wen 407 arr.		6 57			9 0	9 43	10 47				12 59			1 37	
	Afon Wen 407 dep.	6 25	7 0	8 32		9 6	9 50	10 53				1s5			1 45	
55¾	Abererch			8 38		9 12		10 59				1s10			1 51	
57¾	Pwllheli C arr.	6 35	7 10	8 43		9 17	10 0	11 4				1s15			1 57	

Down. Week Days—Continued.	Through Carriages, Manchester (Exchange) to Pwllheli, see pages 391 and 407.	aft	aft	aft	aft	Through Carriages, London (Euston) to Pwllheli, see pages 392 and 407.	aft	Through Carriages, London (Paddington) to Pwllheli, see page 144.	aft	aft	aft	Through Carriages, Liverpool (Lime Street) to Pwllheli, see pages 393 and 407.	aft	aft	Sn mrn
Machynlleth ....dep.		1 22							4 36				5 47		8 50
Dovey Junction ....arr.		1 29							4 43				5 55		
138 Aberystwyth ......dep.		1255							2 40				5 5		
Dovey Junction ¶ ......dep.		1 40		m					4 48				6 5		
Aberdovey		1 54		4 30					5 2				6 20		9 11
Towyn A 946		2 2		4 38					5 10				6 33		9 19
Tonfanau		2 7		4 44					Dd				6 38		
Llwyngwril		2 15		4 52					5 23				6 47		9 32
Fairbourne, for Friog		2 24		5 4					5 32				6 56		9 41
Barmouth Junction 145 arr.		2 27		5 7					...				6 59		
Dolgelley 144, 145 arr.		2 51		6 25					6p25				7 41		
Dolgelley 144, 145 dep.					4 56						6 15			8 50	
Barmouth Junction ....dep.		2 31		5 9	5 16						6 37		7 1	9 10	9 45
Barmouth ¶ arr.		2 36		5 14	5 21				5 40		6 42		7 6	9 15	9 50
Barmouth ¶ dep.		2 40	4 10						5 45	5 55			7 15		
Dyffryn-on-Sea ¶		2 50	4 22							6 7			7 25		
Llanbedr and Pensarn		2 57	4 30							6 15			7 32		
Harlech		3 5	4 39						6 4	6 23			7 39		
Talsarnau		3 13	4 46							6 37			7 50		
Penrhyndeudraeth		3 18	4 50						Bb	6 42			7 55		
Minffordd 949		3 22	4 58						6 20	6 46			7 59		
Portmadoc B ¶ arr.		3 26	5 2						6 24	6 50			8 4		
Portmadoc B ¶ dep.		3 29	5 5						6 31				8 10		
Criccieth		3 39	5 16						6 42				8 21		
Afon Wen 407 arr.		3 47	5 25						6 49				8 28		
Afon Wen 407 dep.		3 52	5 33				6 15		6 55				8 41		
Abererch		...	5 39				Cc		7 1				8 47		
Pwllheli C arr.		4 2	5 45				6 25		7 6				8 52		

A ¼ mile to Tal-y-llyn Co.'s Station.
Aa Stops to set down on notice being given to the Guard.
B Station for Borthygest and Beddgelert; ¼ mile to Festiniog Co.'s Sta.
Bb Stops to set down from Ruabon or beyond on notice being given to the Guard at Barmouth.
C Station for Nevin and Morfa Nevin (7 miles).
Cc Stops to set down from the L.M.&S. Line on notice being given to the Guard at Afon Wen.

Dd Stops to set down from Crewe, Shrewsbury, and beyond, on notice being given to the Guard at Dovey Junction.

¶ "Halts" at Gogarth, between Dovey Junc. and Aberdovey; at Llanaber and at Talybont, between Barmouth and Dyffryn-on-Sea; at Talwrn Bach, between Dyffryn-on-Sea and Llanbedr and Pensarn; and at Black Rock, between Portmadoc and Criccieth.

m Motor Car, one class only.
n Motor Car, one class only.
p Motor Car, one class only, via Barmouth.
s Saturdays only.

May 1953

Table 189 MACHYNLLETH, TOWYN, BARMOUTH, and PWLLHELI

Week Days

Miles	Station	a.m	a.m (From Bangor dep. 5 30 a.m page 517)	a.m	a.m	a.m	a.m	a.m	a.m	p.m (RC from Liverpool (Lime St.) dep. 7E50 (7S42) a.m. From Bangor dep. 11E35 (11S30) a.m. page 517)	a.m
—	Machynlleth ....dep				6 50		8 10				1045
3¾	Dovey Junction..... arr						8 17				11 0
—	1 4 Aberystwyth.....dep						7 10				9 55
—	Dovey Junction .... dep						8 25				1110
5½	Gogarth Halt						8 29				1114
7	Abertafol Halt						8 35				1120
9	Penhelig Halt				7 11		8 40				1125
9¾	Aberdovey				7 15		8 43				1129
13½	Towyn				7 27		8 51				1138
15¾	Tonfanau				7 33		8 58				1145
18	Llangelynin Halt						9 2				1149
20	Llwyngwril				7 41		9 8				1156
22¾	Fairbourne				7 48		9 15				12 5
23¾	Barmouth Junction. arr				7 51		9 18				12 8
33	187 Dolgelley arr					③	9n51				1 37
	187 Dolgelley dep					8 30		9 30	1138		
—	Barmouth Junction. dep				7 52	8 52	9 19	10 3	12 3		1210
25½	Barmouth arr				7 57	8 57	9 24	10 8	12 8		1215
	Barmouth dep				8 10		9 27				
27	Llanaber Halt						9 31				
29¼	Talybont Halt						9 35				
30½	Dyffryn-Ardudwy				8 18		9 39				
32¾	Talwrn Bach Halt				8 24		9 44				
33½	Llanbedr and Pensarn				8 30		9 47				
34	Llandanwg Halt				8 32		9 49				
36	Harlech				8 41		9 56				
38½	Tygwyn Halt				8 46		10 1				
39½	Talsarnau				8 49		10 4				
40¾	Llandecwyn Halt				8 53		10 8				
41½	Penrhyndeudraeth				8 58		1014				
42½	Minffordd				9 2		1018				
44¾	Pertmadoc arr				9 6		1023				
	Pertmadoc dep	6 0		7 40	9 8		1025				
48¾	Black Rock Halt						1032				
49¾	Criccieth	6 9		7 49	9 18		1037				
53	Afon Wen arr	6 15		7 56	9 24		1042				
	Afon Wen dep	6 25	7 9	8 5	9 25		1045			1255	
54½	Penychain D	6 28	7 12	8 8	9 28		1048			1258	
55½	Abererch		7 15	8 11	9 32		1052			1 1	
57¾	Pwllheli arr	6 35	7 21	8 17	9 38		1058			1 7	

Miles	Station	p.m	p.m	p.m	p.m (From Bangor dep. 2 52 p.m page 517)	p.m	p.m	p.m	p.m	p.m	p.m	p.m	p.m	Sundays a.m
—	Machynlleth ....dep			1 15			3 35			5 30		6 55		9 0
3¾	Dovey Junction..... arr			1 22			3 42			5 37		7 2		
—	1 4 Aberystwyth.....dep			1250			2 30			4 50		6 0		
—	Dovey Junction .... dep			1 35			3 43			5 39		7 5		
5½	Gogarth Halt			1 39			Uu					7 11		
7	Abertafol Halt			1 45			3 52			5 48		Uu		
9	Penhelig Halt			1 50			3 57			5 54		7 19		9 19
9¾	Aberdovey			1 53			4 1			5 58		7 24		9 23
13½	Towyn			2 0			4 9			6 9		7 32		9 31
15¾	Tonfanau			2 6			4 14			6 14		7 38		9 36
18	Llangelynin Halt			2 10			4 18					7 43		
20	Llwyngwril			2 20			4 22			6 22		7 49		9 44
22¾	Fairbourne			2 27			4 29			6 30		7 57		9 52
23¾	Barmouth Junction. arr			2 29			4 33			6 32		8 0		9 55
33	187 Dolgelley arr		③	3 2			6n12			7 46	③	9§16		
	187 Dolgelley dep		1 45					4 16	5 20	5 20	6 18		9 3	
—	Barmouth Junction. dep		2 7	2 30			4 34	4 40	5 40	6 33	6 40	8 2	9 30	9 56
25½	Barmouth arr		2 12	2 35			4 39	4 45	5 45	6 38	6 45	8 7	9 35	10 1
	Barmouth dep	1220		2 40		3 45		4 50	5 55	6 50		8 12		
27	Llanaber Halt	1224				3 49		4 54		6 54		8 16		
29¼	Talybont Halt	1229				3 53		4 58		6 58		8 21		
30½	Dyffryn-Ardudwy	1233		2 49		3 57		5 7		7 2		8 29		
32¾	Talwrn Bach Halt	1238				4 2		5 12		7 7		8 34		
33½	Llanbedr and Pensarn	1243		2 56		4 6		5 16		7 10		8 37		
34	Llandanwg Halt	1245				4 8		5 19				8 39		
36	Harlech	1252		3 5		4 14		5 25	6 25	7 18		8 46		
38½	Tygwyn Halt	1257				4 18		5 29				8 51		
39½	Talsarnau	1 0		3 11		4 21		5 32		7 24		8 54		
40¾	Llandecwyn Halt	1 2				4 25		5 37				8 58		
41½	Penrhyndeudraeth	1 7		3 17		4 31		5 41	6 36	7 30		9 2		
42½	Minffordd	1 11		3 21		4 35		5 46		7 34		9 6		
44¾	Pertmadoc arr	1 15		3 2[illegible]		4 40		5 51	6 42	7 39		9 11		
	Pertmadoc dep	1 18		3 23		4 44		5 55	6 43	8 15		9 15		
48¾	Black Rock Halt	1 25				4 52								
49¾	Criccieth	1 30		3 38		4 57		6 4	6 52	8 24		9 25		
53	Afon Wen arr	1 36		3 44		5 3		6 9	6 57	8 30		9 31		
	Afon Wen dep	1 49		3 58	4 19	5 5		6 10	6 59	8 35		9 34		
54½	Penychain D	1 52		4 1	4 22	5 8		6 13	7 2	8 38		9 37		
55½	Abererch	1 55		4 4	4 25	5 11		6 16	7 5	8 41				
57¾	Pwllheli arr	2 1		4 10	4 31	5 17		6 22	7 11	8 47		9 45		

D For Pwllheli Holiday Camp.
▮ Third class only

n Third class only on Saturdays
RC Through Carriages

Uu Calls to set down passengers on notice being given by the passenger to the Guard at Dovey Junc.

§ Third class only. on Saturdays.
③ Third class only.

Arrive 10 6 p.m.

MACHYNLLETH, BARMOUTH, and PWLLHELI

March 1938

Miles	Down.		Week Days. mn	mrn	mn	mn	mrn		mrn	mrn Mondays only.	mrn Except Mondays.	mrn		non	mrn		aft	mrn		aft	aft (TC Manchester (Ex.) to Pwllheli, page 506.)		aft
	Machynlleth	dep.	..	6 10	..	..	8 15	..	..	..	..	..	..	..	1031	..	..	..	..	..	1 17	..	..
3¾	Dovey Junction	arr.	..	..	..	..	8 21	..	..			..	..	..	1037	..	..	..	..	..	1 23	..	..
—	144 Aberystwyth	dep.	..	..	..	..	7 50	..	..			..	..	..	1015	..	..	..	..	..	1 0	..	..
—	Dovey Junction ¶	dep.	..	..	..	..	8 31	..	..			..	..	..	1055	..	..	..	..	..	1 37	..	..
9¾	Aberdovey		..	6 32	..	..	8 49	..	..			..	..	..	1113	..	..	..	..	..	1 55	..	..
13½	Towyn A 1084		..	6 39	..	..	8 56	..	..			..	..	..	1120	..	..	..	..	..	2 2	..	..
15¾	Tonfanau ¶		..	Aa	..	..	9 1	..	..			..	..	..	1125	..	..	..	..	..	2 7	..	..
20	Llwyngwril		..	6 52	..	..	9 10	..	..			..	..	..	1134	..	..	..	..	..	2 15	..	..
22½	Fairbourne, for Friog		..	7 0	..	..	9 17	..	..			..	..	..	1142	..	..	..	..	..	2 23	..	..
23¾	Barmouth Junction 149	arr.	..	7 3	..	..	9 20	..	..			..	..	..	1145	..	..	..	..	..	2 26	..	..
33	Dolgelley 148, 149	arr.	..	8 9	..	m	9N53	..	..	m	m	..	..	..	N 1257	..	..		..	m	3 3	..	..
		dep.	..	..	7 0	850	..	..	9 40	1030	1040	..	..	..	..	..	..	1132	..	1 45	..	..	3 15
—	Barmouth Junction	dep.	..	7 4	722	911	9 21	..	10 5	1056	11 5	..	..	..	1146	..	..	1154	..	2 7	2 29	..	3 37
25½	Barmouth ¶	arr.	..	7 9	727	915	9 26	..	1010	11 1	1110	m	..	..	1151	..	..	1159	..	2 12	2 34	..	3 42
		dep.	..		740		9 29	..	..	..	..	1113	..	..	..	..	..	12 5	..	..	2 37	..	..
30½	Dyffryn-on-Sea ¶		..	Stop	748	Stp	9 40	..	..	..	..	1125	..	..	..	..	..	1215	..	..	2 49	..	..
33¾	Llanbedr and Pensarn ¶		..	..	754	..	9 48	..	..	..	..	1132	..	..	..	..	..	1224	..	..	2 57	..	..
36	Harlech ¶		..	..	8 2	..	9 56	..	..	..	..	1142	..	..	..	..	..	1233	..	..	3 5	..	..
39¼	Talsarnau ¶		..	..	810	..	10 4	..	..	..	..	..	..	..	..	..	..	1242	..	..	3 13	..	..
41½	Penrhyndeudraeth		..	..	816	..	1010	..	..	..	..	..	..	..	..	..	..	1250	..	..	3 19	..	..
42½	Minffordd 1075a		..	..	820	..	1016	..	..	..	..	..	..	..	..	..	..	1255	..	..	3 23	..	..
44½	Portmadoc B ¶	arr.	..	mrn	825	mn	10 2	..	..	..	..	..	..	..	..	..	..	1 0	..	..	3 28	..	..
		dep.	..	6 40	830	9 0	1023	..	..	..	..	..	..	12 0	..	..	..	1 5	..	..	3 29	..	..
49¾	Criccieth		..	6 49	840	9 8	1034	..	..	..	..	..	..	1211	..	..	..	1 17	..	..	3 38	..	..
53	Afon Wen 515	arr.	..	6 55	846	915	1041	..	..	..	..	..	..	1218	..	..	..	1 25	..	..	3 44	..	..
		dep.	622	6 57	847	918	1043	..	..	..	..	..	..	1222	..	..	1 10	1 31	..	..	3 48	..	..
55¾	Abererch		..	7 2	853	923	1049	..	..	..	..	..	..	1228	..	..	Aa	1 37	..	..	3 53	..	..
57¾	Pwllheli C	arr.	632	7 8	859	929	1055	..	..	..	..	..	..	1234	..	..	1 20	1 43	..	..	3 59	..	..

Down.		Week Days—Continued. aft (TC London (E.) to Pwllheli, pages 506 and 515.)	aft		(TC London (P.) and Birkenhead to Pwllheli, page 148.)	aft S		aft E (TC London (P.) & Birkenhead to Pwllheli, p. 148.)		aft S		aft	aft		aft		aft		aft	S	Suns.	mrn	
Machynlleth	dep.		3 24	..		..	..	..	..	..	..	426	..	..	534	..	..	..	..	8 0	..	8 25	..
Dovey Junction	arr.		3 30	..		..	..	..	..	..	..	433	..	..	540	..	..	..	..	8 6	..	..	..
144 Aberystwyth	dep.		2 50	..		..	..	..	..	..	..	..	..	..	5 5	..	..	..	..	7 30	..	..	..
Dovey Junction ¶	dep.		3 35	..		..	..	..	..	..	..	438	..	..	6 0	..	..	..	..	8 20	..	..	..
Aberdovey			3 52	..		..	..	..	..	..	..	455	..	..	618	..	..	..	..	8 37	..	8 47	..
Towyn A 1084			4 8	..		..	..	..	..	..	..	5 2	..	..	629	..	..	..	..	8 44	..	8 54	..
Tonfanau ¶			4 15	..		..	..	..	..	..	..	5 7	..	..	634	..	..	..	..	8 49	..	8 59	..
Llwyngwril			4 24	..		..	..	..	..	..	..	515	..	..	643	..	..	..	..	8 57	..	9 7	..
Fairbourne, for Friog			4 33	..		..	..	..	..	..	..	523	..	..	651	..	..	..	..	9 5	..	9 15	..
Barmouth Junction 149	arr.		4 36	..		..	..	..	..	..	..	526	..	..	653	..	..	..	..	9 8	..	9 17	..
Dolgelley 148, 149	arr.		..	..		..	..	..	..	..	..	615	m	..	747	..	..	..	..	N 1042	..	..	..
	dep.		..	..		4 26	..	4 43	..	4 55	..	..	6 25	..	..	..	..	..	8 38	..	..	..	..
Barmouth Junction	dep.		4 39	..		4 47	..	5 6	..	5 18	..	527	6 49	..	654	..	..	..	9 0	9 9	..	9 18	..
Barmouth ¶	arr.		4 44	..		4 53	..	5 11	..	5 23	..	532	6 54	..	659	..	..	..	9 5	9 14	..	9 23	..
	dep.	4 8	..	..		5 0	..	5 15	..		..	540	..	..	..	..	715	..	..	9 25	..	..	..
Dyffryn-on-Sea ¶		4 20	..	..		Bb	..	Bb	..	Stop	..	553	..	..	..	..	727	..	..	9 39	..	..	..
Llanbedr and Pensarn ¶		4 28	..	..		Bb	..	Bb	..	..	..	6 1	..	..	..	..	735	..	..	9 47	..	..	..
Harlech ¶		4 36	..	..		5 21	..	5 36	..	..	..	612	..	..	..	..	746	..	..	9 55	..	..	..
Talsarnau ¶		4 44	..	..		Bb	..	Bb	..	..	..	620	..	..	..	..	754	..	..	10 3	..	..	..
Penrhyndeudraeth		4 52	..	..		Bb	..	Bb	..	..	..	628	..	..	..	..	759	..	..	1011	..	..	..
Minffordd 1075a		4 57	..	..		..	..	..	..	..	..	632	..	..	..	..	8 4	..	..	1015	..	..	..
Portmadoc B ¶	arr.	5 2	..	..		5 43	..	6 2	..	..	..	637	..	..	..	..	8 9	..	..	1020	..	..	..
	dep.	5 6	..	..		5 45	..	6 3	..	..	..	639	..	..	..	..	810	..	..	..	..	..	..
Criccieth		5 18	..	..		5 54	..	6 12	..	aft	..	648	..	..	..	..	819	..	..	..	..	..	..
Afon Wen ¶ 515	arr.	5 24	..	..		..	..	6 18	..	S	..	654	..	..	..	..	825	..	..	..	..	..	..
	dep.	5 33	..	..		..	..	6 20	..	6 20	..	656	..	..	..	..	828	..	..	..	..	..	..
Abererch		5 39	..	..		..	..	..	..	..	..	7 2	..	..	..	..	834	..	..	..	..	..	..
Pwllheli C	arr.	5 45	..	..		6 10	..	6 30	..	6 30	..	7 8	..	..	..	..	840	..	..	..	..	..	..

A ½ mile to Tal-y-llyn Co.'s Station. Aa Stops to set down on notice being given to the Guard. Bb Stops to set down from beyond Ruabon on notice to Guard at Barmouth. B Station for Borthygest and Beddgelert: ½ mile to Festiniog Company's Station. C Sta. for Nevin & Morfa Nevin (7 mls.). E or E Except Saturdays. m or N One class only. S or S Sats. only. TC Thro Carrs. ¶ "Halts" at Gogarth, at Abertafol and at Penhelig, between Dovey J. and Aberdovey; at Llangelynin, between Tonfanau and Llwyngwril; at Llanaber and at Talybont, between Barmouth and Dyffryn-on-Sea; at Talwrn Bach, between Dyffryn-on-Sea and Llanbedr & Pensarn: at Llandanwg, between Llanbedr & Pensarn & Harlech; at Tygwyn, between Harlech & Talsarnau; at Llandecwyn, between Talsarnau & Penrhyndeudraeth; at Black Rock, between Portmadoc and Criccieth; and at Penychain, between Afon Wen & Abererch.

Shrewsbury — Pwllheli
Second Class only

May 1984

Miles		Mondays to Saturdays	A	C WO	D	A	E SX	G SO		SX	J SO	K SO	L SX		N	A	P	Sundays (1 July to 26 August) Q
0	Shrewsbury d	0410	..	..	0744b	..	0915	1000	1046	..	..	1311	..	1439	1648	1853c	1853c	0948
—	Aberystwyth d	0515b	0715	..	0715	..	1010	1010	1135	1400c	1400c	1400c	..	..	1705e	1912	1912	1055c
61	Machynlleth 75 d	0719	0816	..	0923	..	1046	1134	1235	1412	1412	1500	1518	1630	1828	2028	2028	1118
65	Dovey Junction 75 d	..		..		..			..	1428	1428	1507		..	1850	2047	2047	1125
66¼	Gogarth d	..	0826x	..		..			..	..				..				..
68¼	Abertafol d	..	0830x	..		..			..	..				..				..
70	Penhelig d	0737x	0835x	..	0941x	..	1104x	1153x	1253x	1440x	1440x	1519x	1536x	1648x	1902x	2059x	2059x	1137x
71	Aberdovey d	0741	0839	..	0945	..	1108	1156	1257	1443	1443	1522	1540	1652	1905	2102	2102x	1141
74¼	Tywyn d	0747	0846	..	0951	..	1114	1210	1303	1450	1450	1529	1550	1702	1912	2109	2109	1147
77	Tonfanau d	..	0850x	..	0956x	..			..	1454x		1533x	1555x	1706x				..
79½	Llangelynin d	..	0855x	..	1000x	..			..	1459x	1459x	1538x	1559x	1711x				..
81¼	Llwyngwril d	0757x	0859x	..	1005x	..	1124x	1220x	1313x	1503x	1503x	1542x	1604x	1715x	1921x	2118x	2118x	1157x
84	Fairbourne d	0805	0907	..	1013	..	1132	1228	1321	1511	1511	1550	1612	1723	1929	2126	2126	1205
85	Morfa Mawddach d	0807x	0910x	..	1015x	..	1134x	1230x	1323x	1514x	1514x	1553x	1614x	1726x	1932x	2129x	2129x	1207x
86½	Barmouth a	0813	0916	..	1021	..	1140	1236	1329	1520	1520	1559	1620	1732	1938	2135	2135	1213
—	d	0817	..	..	1030	1030	1145	1236	1333	1521	1521	1617	..	1805	1938	..	2135	..
88	Llanaber d	0820x	..	..	1033x	1033x			..	1524x	1524x	1621x	..	1808x	1941x	..	2138x	..
90¼	Talybont d	0824x	..	..	1037x	1037x	1151x	1243x	1339x	1528x	1528x	1625x	..	1812x	1945x	..	2142x	..
91¼	Dyffryn Ardudwy d	0827x	..	..	1040x	1040x	1154x	1246x	1342x	1531x	1531x	1628x	..	1815x	1948x	..	2145x	..
93¾	Llanbedr d	0832x	..	..	1045x	1045x	1159x	1250x	1347x	1536x	1536x	1632x	..	1820x	1953x	..	2150x	..
94¼	Pensarn d	0834x	..	..	1047x	1047x			..	1538x	1538x	1634x	..	1822x	1955x	..	2152x	..
95¼	Llandanwg d	0836x	..	..	1049x	1049x	1202x	1254x	1350x	1540x	1540x	1636x	..	1824x	1957x	..	2154x	..
97¼	Harlech d	0847	..	..	1100	1100	1208	1303	1356	1549	1549	1644	..	1832	2008	..	2202	..
99½	Tygwyn d	0852x	..	..	1105x	1105x			..	1553x	1553x	1648x	..	1836x	2013x	..		..
100¼	Talsarnau d	0854x	..	..	1107x	1107x	1214x	1309x	1402x	1556x	1556x	1651x	..	1839x	2015x	..	2207x	..
101½	Llandecwyn d	0857x	..	..	1110x	1110x			..	1559x	1559x	1654x	..	1842x	2018x	..		..
102¼	Penrhyndeudraeth d	0900	..	..	1113	1113	1219	1314	1407	1602	1602	1657	..	1845	2021	..	2213	..
103¾	Minffordd § d	0904	..	..	1117	1117	1223	1318	1411	1606	1606	1701	..	1849	2025	..	2217	..
106	Porthmadog d	0908	..	..	1121	1121	1242	1322	1415	1610	1610	1711	..	1853	2029	..	2221	..
111	Criccieth d	0917	..	..	1130	1130	1251	1331	1424	1619	1619	1720	..	1902	2038	..	2230	..
115¼	Penychain ‡ d	0924x	..	1000	1137x	1137x	1258x	1338x	1431x	1626x	1626x	1727x	..	1909x	2045x	..	2237x	..
117	Abererch d	0927x	..	1003x	1140x	1140x	1301x	1341x	1434x	1629x	1629x	1730x	..	1912x	2048x	..	2240x	..
118½	Pwllheli a	0932	..	1007	1145	1145	1305	1346	1439	1633	1633	1735	..	1916	2053	..	2244	..

N Until 27 October

P Saturdays 26 May and 14 July, and Mondays to Saturdays 28 May to 2 June and 16 July to 1 September

Q From Birmingham New Street dep 08 42 (Table 74)

U Mondays to Fridays 28 May to 1 June and 16 July to 31 August to Wolverhampton arr 1317 (Table 74)

V Mondays to Saturdays until 19 May and 4 June to 6 July and from 3 September, Mondays to Fridays 21 May to 25 May and 9 July to 13 July

A Mondays to Saturdays until 19 May, 4 June to 7 July and from 3 September, and Mondays to Fridays 21 to 25 May and 9 to 13 July

C 30 May and 18 July to 29 August

D Saturdays 26 May and 14 July and Mondays to Saturdays 28 May to 2 June and 16 July to 1 September

E 28 May to 1 June and 16 July to 31 August

G 26 May to 15 September. From Birmingham New Street dep. 0843 (Table 74)

J 19 May, 9 June to 7 July and from 8 September

K 26 May and 2 June and 14 July to 1 September

L Until 25 May, 4 June to 13 July and from 3 September

Y Saturdays 26 May and 14 July also Mondays to Saturdays 28 May to 2 June and 16 July to 1 September. Saturdays to Birmingham New Street arr 1553 (Table 74)

Z To Birmingham New Street arr 2114 (Table 74)

b Mondays and Saturdays only

c Change at Dovey Junction

e Change at Machynlleth and Dovey Junction

f Mondays to Fridays 28 May to 1 June and 16 July to 31 August. Saturdays Throughout and Mondays to Fridays until 25 May, 4 June to 13 July and from 3 September, is connection arr 1222

g Saturdays

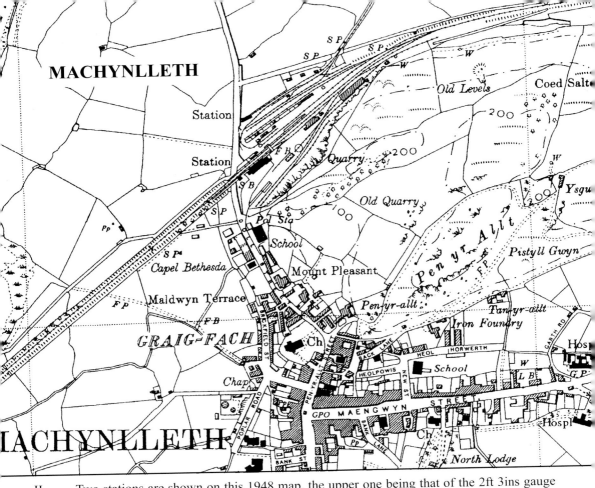

MACHYNLLETH

Station

Station

Capel Bethesda

Maldwyn Terrace

GRAIG-FACH

Chap

IACHYNLLETH

Old Levels

Coed Salt

Quarry

Old Quarry

School

Mount Pleasant

Pen-yr-allt

Pen yr Allt

Pistyll Gwyn

Ysgu

Tan-yr-allt

Iron Foundry

School

Hos

G.P.

Hospl

North Lodge

GPO MAENGWYN STREET

BANK ST

II.   Two stations are shown on this 1948 map, the upper one being that of the 2ft 3ins gauge Corris Railway, which closed that year. The scale is 12ins to 1 mile.

1.   The main buildings were recorded as having been built from stone excavated from Talerddig Cutting. They are seen from the south on an undated postcard. (J.Evans/SLS coll.)

2.　　　Pulling into the up platform on 15th August 1913 is 4-4-0 no. 70. It had been constructed by Sharp Stewart in 1894. The up side has always had minimal shelter. The up expresses in 1913 were at 10.2am, 1.2pm and 1.58pm. (K.Nunn/LCGB coll.)

3.　　　At the down platform sometime after 1923 is ex-CR 0-6-0 no. 87. It had been built in 1899 by Neilson and is carrying the GWR no. 884. On the right is West Box, which had 13 levers; East Box had 23. (P.Q.Treloar coll.)

4.	The west end of the engine shed and coal stage are seen in October 1959, along with 4-4-0 no. 9017 out of use, on the right. It is seen in happier times in picture 116. (P.J.Kelley)

5.	A panorama from the top of the cliff in the previous photograph in 1965 includes a DMU and a turntable, which was 55ft in length and replaced a 50ft one. (C.C.Green/G.Williams)

6.   No. 78003 stands at the east end of the shed on 12th July 1966, the year in which steam ended. This building had been completed in 1863 and the three-road extension was added ten years later. (R.Ruffell/M.J.Stretton coll.)

7.   Lower yard was used for general goods until about 1974. In the centre distance is the Corris Railway terminus, which was used by passengers until 1931. The photograph is from about 1965. (C.C.Green/G.Williams)

8.   The class 101 DMU on the 19.00 from Aberystwyth on 1st June 1979 is approaching the train from Pwllheli, prior to joining it and forming the service to Shrewsbury. The track in the distance was laid near the 1859 alignment of the Corris Railway to Derwenlas Wharf. (T.Heavyside)

9.　　The panorama from the footbridge on 24th June 1981 has the re-roofed engine shed in the distance and the 50-lever signal box at the end of the up platform. It replaced two boxes on 27th March 1960. The class 101 DMU is waiting to follow an Aberystwyth train to Dovey Junction. (T.Heavyside)

Other views of this station and the next can be seen in our *Newtown to Aberystwyth* album.

10.　　The Pwllheli portion of the 12.02 to Birmingham New Street waits for its other half on 1st September 2008. It is a class 158 DMU. Most trains continued to Birmingham International from 2009. The siding leads to the Train Care Facility. (V.Mitchell)

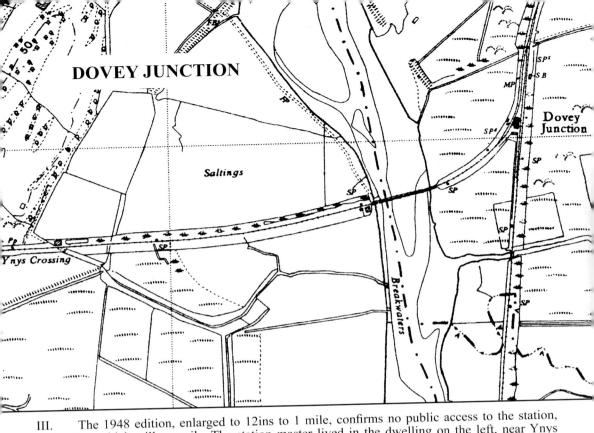

DOVEY JUNCTION

Saltings

Ynys Crossing

Breakwaters

Dovey Junction

III.   The 1948 edition, enlarged to 12ins to 1 mile, confirms no public access to the station, a situation which still prevails. The station master lived in the dwelling on the left, near Ynys Crossing, and had to cross the River Dovey in which the dots and dashes of the county boundary are shown.

11.   No. 4599 had just descended the incline from the bridge with the 9.35am from Barmouth on 25th August 1948. Roses, refreshments and resting places greeted travellers in those days. (H.C.Casserley)

12.   Seats were at a premium when trains terminated here. This undated view includes a fingerboard showing ABERDOVEY, TOWYN AND BARMOUTH. The station was named Glandovey Junction until 1904. (SLS coll.)

13.   A train bound for Barmouth runs in and above its rear coach can be seen the roof of the signal box, which had 52 levers and was in use from 1890 until 1959. The locomotive is 4-4-0 no. 9004. (W.A.Camwell/SLS coll.)

14.　　No. 9009 departs for Machynlleth, while a goods train from the Barmouth line waits in the loop. The 9000 class was introduced by the GWR in 1936. No picture dates are available. The left platform takes nine coaches and the right one five. (W.A.Camwell/SLS coll.)

15.　　The Barmouth platform was recorded on 31st July 1976, together with the replacement signal box. This functioned from 22nd February 1959 until 22nd October 1988. It had 65 levers in its frame. The new station buildings arrived in 1956 and they lasted until 1993. The booking office is in the centre and the waiting room is behind the sign. They were disused for more than ten years before demolition. (D.A.Thompson)

16.　　Running down from the 152yd-long bridge on 25th June 1981 is the 08.00 from Pwllheli. The DMU is a class 101. The bridge once had a lifting span to allow sailing barges to reach Derwenlas Wharf. It was last used in 1890 and became fixed in 1914. The bridgekeeper lived in the house on the right. (T.Heavyside)

17.   The 11.20 class 150 from Pwllheli to Machynlleth departs on 12th August 1989. The junction points are out of view, as the low area seen is prone to flood water which is not ideal for electric point motors. The track and platforms were raised in 2008 and the down loop was restored. Much ground settlement had taken place. (T.Heavyside)

18.   Seen on the delicate bridge on the same day is no. 37426 with the 09.40 Pwllheli to Euston. There are 21 spans; most are on timber trestles. The steel spans on the right date from 1914 and no. 37421 derailed at the north end of them on 26th August 1991, which ended class 37 haulage on these trains. (T.Heavyside)

GOGARTH

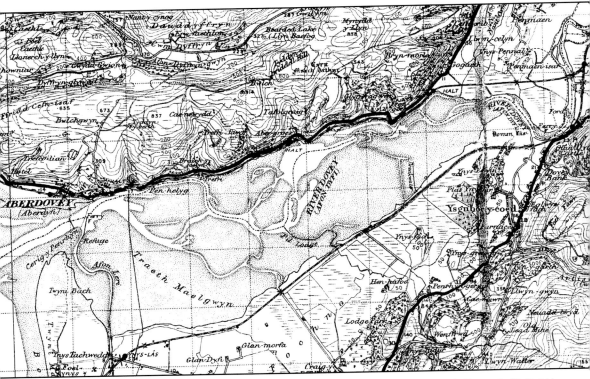

IV.　　The 1ins to 1 mile edition of 1947 has Dovey Junction top right and Gogarth Halt 1½ miles to the west of it. Abertafol Halt is a further 1½ miles. Lower left is Ynyslas from where the railway's ferry service operated to Aberdovey in 1863-67.

19.　　The halt opened on 9th July 1923 and 2-6-2T no. 82009 is seen departing west in May 1962. The line across the marshes had been subject to settlement. (C.L.Caddy)

20. The path through the grass gives an indication of the limited traffic at this location; it was mostly school children. Cattle traffic was handled at a ramp one mile east of the halt at Ynys Crossing between 1934 and about 1950. (C.C.Green/G.Williams)

21. The 16.01 Tywyn to Machynlleth was formed of a class 108 unit on 27th September 1971. Closure came on 14th May 1984, due to decay of the structure. (C.L.Caddy)

WEST OF GOGARTH

22.   Frongoch Tunnel is 200yds in length and this is its west portal in 1974. A tramway from Frongoch Quarry had once passed under the bridge. It terminated at a wharf, where slates were loaded onto ships. (R.S.Carpenter)

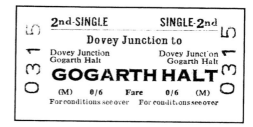

23.   Morfa Bach Tunnel follows and it is 219 yds long. Seen in about 1960 is its west portal and a short bridge over a tideway. (R.S.Carpenter)

ABERTAFOL

24.   The halt was opened on 18th March 1935 close to an existing cottage used by a ganger. There is a superb vista across the estuary from this location. (GWR)

25.   The halt is obscured by the leading coach, but the cottage roof is visible. No. 9003 is piloting a BR class 2 2-6-0 through the stunning scenery in about 1955. (M.Whitehouse coll.)

26.   The cottage was erected in 1887 using timber salvaged during the rebuilding of Barmouth Bridge. The path from the platform climbed steeply immediately behind the building. (C.C.Green/G.Williams)

27.   The 11.54 Dovey Junction to Pwllheli passes on 2nd October 1971, formed of a class 101 DMU. The platform was later deemed unsafe and closed on the same day as Gogarth, 14th May 1984. It was only used by school pupils in its final months. (C.L.Caddy)

PENHELIG

28.   The third tunnel on the route was called Penhelig and is seen from the halt of that name on 16th June 1974. The bore was 191yds long and had proved unstable more than once. The bridge passes over the main road. (R.S.Carpenter)

29.   All the halts lost their suffixes in 1968 and this is the only one to remain open into the 21st century. It is situated at the east end of the town and came into use on 8th May 1933. This eastward view is from May 1967. (R.F.Roberts/SLS coll.)

30.   Using the tunnel numbering commonly employed, this is No. 4 or Craig-y-Don Tunnel, its length being 533yds. This was the busiest of the halts and was provided with a ticket office. The photograph is from 5th October 1972. (C.L.Caddy)

31.   The 11.54 from Dovey Junction is seen on the same day, as the nation's "Tunnel of Trees" encroaches and ruins the view. A porter was once available for delivery of parcels and luggage. The platform takes three coaches. The DMU is a class 108. (C.L.Caddy)

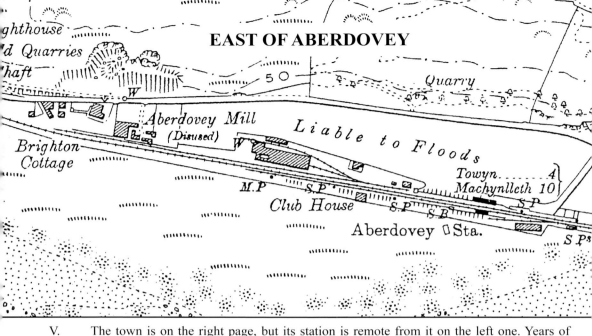

V.   The town is on the right page, but its station is remote from it on the left one. Years of complaint resulted in Penhelig Halt being provided, just beyond the right border. Penhelig Tunnel is behind much of the town and the line emerges from it near the quarry. This 1901 map is scaled at 12ins to 1 mile. A siding runs to the mill on the left, which lasted until 1896.

32.   A train for Pwllheli has just emerged from Penhelig Tunnel and is about to pass over the coast road on 1st August 1955. The branch to Aberdovey Harbour is in the distance. (H.F.Wheeller/R.S.Carpenter coll.)

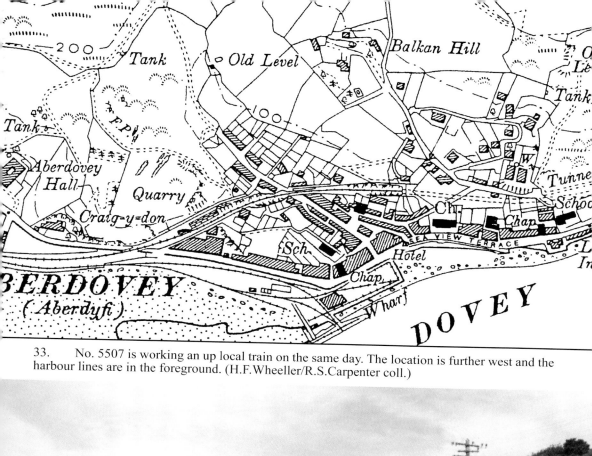

33.　　No. 5507 is working an up local train on the same day. The location is further west and the harbour lines are in the foreground. (H.F.Wheeller/R.S.Carpenter coll.)

34.   Continuing west, we approach the station, where the harbour route rises to join the main line. The building on the left is the weigh house. A train from Pwllheli passes in May 1963, hauled by 0-6-0 no. 2276. We will examine the branch and goods yard before visiting the station. (C.L.Caddy)

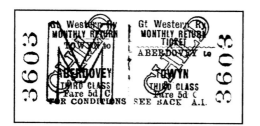

ABERDOVEY HARBOUR

35.   To operate the isolated section between 1863 and 1867, motive power had to be ferried across the Dovey from Ynyslas. The first was this Manning Wardle product of 1862. It had been purchased by the contractor and became CR no. 17. It is on the quay after arrival. (C.C.Green coll.)

36.   This pre-1900 panorama can be located on the map. The wharf and cattle pens are in the foreground, with the jetty beyond. A schooner is moored to it. Local cattle traffic used pens west of the station. (C.C.Green coll.)

37.   The jetty and schooner are on the left, together with a ferry boat, complete with sail. CAM RYS appears on a wagon on the quay. Sidings were retained as a goods yard until 4th May 1964, but latterly, traffic was mainly coal for local use. (P.Q.Treloar coll.)

38.   Pictured at the harbour on 18th July 1912 is no. 50, a Sharp Stewart built for the CR in 1891. It became GWR no. 1110. (H.W.Burman/G.Williams coll.)

39.　CR no. 79 was photographed at the same location on 12th July 1915. It was completed by Vulcan Foundry in 1895 and was numbered 882 by the GWR. (P.Q.Treloar coll.)

40.　The town was unusual for the Cambrian Coast in being south facing. This postcard view eastwards has tracks on both sides. The seafront sidings were a serious hindrance to the development of the town as a resort, as was the remoteness of the station from it. (P.Q.Treloar coll.)

41.   Two views of the jetty date from about the mid-1920s. The anticipated extensive traffic to Ireland did not develop to any great extent. The SS *Telephone* was recorded at the damaged remnants of the quay. (T.Walsh coll.)

42.   A rail-mounted steam crane arrived in 1885 and lasted until 1923. A grain shed and two warehouses were built on the quay and some trade with Waterford continued until about 1900. Occasional loads came and went, the last being cement inwards in December 1939. (T.Walsh coll.)

ABERDOVEY

43.　　A wooden shed sufficed until 1872, when brick buildings were completed. Seen in about 1912 are facilities created in 1910, using the canopy from Pwllheli's first station. (SLS coll.)

44.　　CR no. 28 came from Sharp Stewart in 1863, but did not last to become GWR property. Early features include a four-wheeled tender and a jack. There were seven employees in the 1930s at this location. (H.W.Burman/P.Q.Treloar coll.)

45.   Standing in front of the signal box are portable steps, which were provided in 1942. The "Cambrian Radio Cruise" is seen headed by 2-6-0 no. 46445, but no date was recorded for this or the next view. They are probably from 1961. (A.J.B.Dodd/P.Chancellor coll.)

46.   No. 2247 is carrying the "Cambrian Coast Express" headboard on the portion from Pwllheli. The driver would face a 25mph speed limit on the curves ahead. The town had 1112 residents in 1961 and a gas supply from 1868. The works was about a mile west of the town centre, close to the railway. It never had a siding, but the supply pipe ran in CR land. (A.J.B.Dodd/P.Chancellor coll.)

47.   Seen in May 1964, the signal box (centre) had 20 levers. Beyond it is the golf club house. The crossing was used by passengers, as no footbridge was ever provided. The photographer is on the end-loading dock. (C.L.Caddy)

Aberdovey	1923	1929	1930	1933
Passenger tickets issued	28292	23508	22770	23643
Season tickets issued	100	141	186	160
Parcels forwarded	13519	11760	12001	12585
Minerals forwarded (tons)	428	623	856	1629
General goods forwarded (tons)	683	1027	473	1403
Coal and coke received (tons)	431	761	633	227
Other minerals received (tons)	1417	1827	1266	1992
General goods received (tons)	1460	1153	1332	813
Trucks of livestock handled	21	25	36	32

48.   The gates on the left gave access to the dock provided for the horse-drawn carriages of the wealthy. There was another siding serving the building in the right background. It was used successively for creosoting timber, concrete products and repairing camp coaches. (R.G.Nelson/T.Walsh)

49.   Behind the down platform waiting shelter, there had once been a siding and store building for Texas oil products. The signal box and down loop were in use until 28th April 1968 and are seen in June 1968. Staffing ceased on 3rd May 1971. (C.L.Caddy)

50.   The canopy lasted until 1982 and the building was sold. The former is in use on the Bala Lake Railway at Llanuwchllyn. No. 158840 worked the 07.31 Pwllheli to Birmingham New Street on 28th May 2008. The platform will take six coaches. (C.L.Caddy)

Gas Works

Pheasantry

TOWYN

Morfa-bâch

Prest

Capel Bethesda
(Ind.)

Police Station

Tyddyn-du

Wells

HIGH STREET

Capel Ebenezer
(Wes. Meth)

Baptist Chapel

L.B.

W.M.

ATHELSTAN RD.

S.P.

F.B.

r View

Intermediate School

NFORD ROAD

ryn

S.B.

Bryn-dedwydd

S.P.

Isandula Terrace

S.P.

King
Statio

VI. The 1901 map includes the terminus of the
1866 Talyllyn Railway, lower right. The gasworks
(top) was open from 1868 to 1964 and was consuming
around 1000 tons of coal per annum in the late 1930s.
The weighing machine (W.M.) was installed in 1883.
The population was 3576 at the time of the survey and
3930 sixty years later.

51.   Our visit starts with a view from the west in about 1890. The staff numbered three in 1866 and nine in the 1930s. The building was completed in 1870 and track was ballasted over the sleepers for long afterwards. The locomotive is no. 7 *Llanerchydol*. (A.Dudman coll.)

52.   The Talyllyn Railway had a wharf here from the outset and traffic was mainly slate outward. Passengers used its Towyn Pendre station exclusively for almost 50 years, but King's station became Wharf in around 1909 and most trains started here subsequently. The picture is from 1953, two years after the TR had become the first railway preserved by volunteers. The loco is no. 895, a Beyer Peacock of 1908 and originally CR no. 101. (G.Farr)

53.   Slate traffic had ceased in 1950 and the only operable locomotive was the Fletcher Jennings 0-4-0WT *Dolgoch* seen here in 1951, close to the 1924 Alvis 12/50 of General Manager L.T.C.Rolt. Your author (V.M.) was conveyed in this to his first restoration task - see *Talyllyn - 50 years of change*. (J.H.Moss/R.S.Carpenter coll.)

54.   No. 78001 is bound for Pwllheli in August 1961 and is seen from the footbridge. The "waiting shed" (left) was authorised in 1891 and a wooden footbridge followed in 1899. The shed lasted until 1961. Sidings were laid in the distance: Sandilands for Army Volunteers 1903-11 on the south side and one for the gasworks on the north side. This was in use from 1906 until its demise in 1964. (D.K.Jones coll.)

55.   The view in the opposite direction a year later features no. 75020 with the 11.10 from Paddington to Pwllheli. An equally lengthy goods train waits to enter the single line south. The tall shed is the goods shed, the next shed is the cement storage shed and the cement pre-fab shed is the grain shed. We can shed no more light on these - sorry! (R.A.Lumber/D.H.Mitchell)

Towyn	1923	1929	1930	1933
Passenger tickets issued	37889	32127	31584	30938
Season tickets issued	9	32	46	73
Parcels forwarded	19874	18120	17813	19847
Minerals forwarded (tons)	2918	1983	1468	1414
General goods forwarded (tons)	749	443	421	331
Coal and coke received (tons)	2789	3336	3049	2671
Other minerals received (tons)	1577	2417	4744	2764
General goods received (tons)	3187	3075	3143	2811
Trucks of livestock handled	615	618	683	402

56.	It is 27th May 1972 and the 14.10 to Barmouth approaches the 1923 signal box, which had 38 levers and replaced two boxes, which dated from 1891. Only South Box is shown on the map. The "new" box had come from Maidenhead. (E.Wilmshurst)

57.	No. 24086 is seen from the road bridge shunting the goods yard on 13th September 1974. The crossover forms the south end of the loop. On the left is the down refuge siding, which had a short platform once served by the Phoenix Tramway. This was used for conveying building materials to the seafront. (C.L.Caddy)

TYWYN

← 58. The spelling was changed in 1976. The sidings were lifted sometime after this photograph was taken on 24th June 1981. The area continued in use as a coal yard for many years, before being used for a supermarket building. (T.Heavyside)

← 59. The refreshment room had closed in 1915, having been the cause of much friction over drinking on Sundays. The Barmouth to Wolverhampton Sunday train arrives on 20th June 1982, by which time only one room in the building was used. Both platforms would accommodate six cars. Class 101 DMUs are in this and the previous view. The canopy columns were acquired for use at Abergynolwyn station on the TR. (C.L.Caddy)

60.   The 08.28 Wolverhampton to Pwllheli slows to surrender the token on 30th September 1987. The crossing and white stage was used by the signalman serving trains in the other direction. The box closed on 22nd October 1988. (C.L.Caddy)

61.   The down platform is in the distance as no. 150110 displays its new Regional Railways livery on 2nd August 1991, while working the 13.13 from Pwllheli. Adjacent to it is the long headshunt, which had accommodated the Land Cruise train on some nights in the 1980s. The siding at the TR wharf had been lifted in 1984. On the right is the Narrow Gauge Museum. (M.J.Stretton)

62.   The "Cambrian Coast Express" from Machynlleth to Porthmadog arrives on 3rd August 2007, behind 2-6-0 no. 76079. The station windows had been bricked up, but the building was in use as a charity shop. (V.Mitchell)

NORTH OF TYWYN

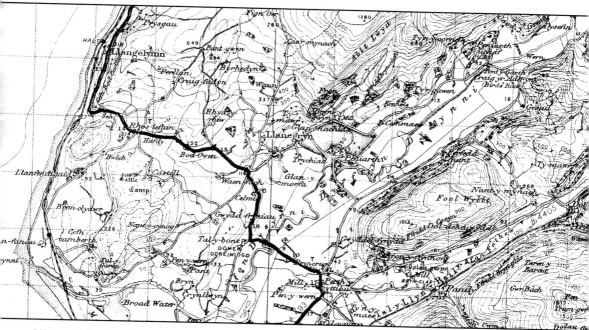

VII.   After leaving Tywyn, the line runs very close to the coast, necessitating prolonged defensive measures. It then passes over the Afon Dysynni (lower left) before meeting the siding from Tal-y-Gareg Quarry. Both are marked on this 1947 map at 1ins to 1 mile. The track was in use from 1907 to about 1953 and there was a public goods siding to the south of its junction from January 1896 to November 1963.

63.   The first bridge over the Dysynni had 24 timber trestles on improperly sunk piles, but it lasted until 1911, when it was replaced by this 114yd-long steel structure, made in Chepstow. The Army built a road bridge north of it and this was in public use in the 1970s, but has long gone. This view north is from 1965. (C.C.Green/G.Williams)

TONFANAU

64.　　The station appeared in the timetable from July to September 1896 and then continuously from July 1903. It had a staff of two in the 1930s and was subject to very heavy traffic in the 1940s, due to the establishment of an Army range nearby. This view north is from 1964, with only the LADIES ROOM being identified. Its access was through the waiting room. Electric lighting came in 1946 and only one train a day, each way, called for many years latterly. (Stations UK)

Tonfanau	1923	1929	1930	1933
Passenger tickets issued	6061	4657	5026	4802
Season tickets issued	60	26	25	28
Parcels forwarded	799	775	960	507
Minerals forwarded (tons)	12023	24720	22199	11622
General goods forwarded (tons)	12	18	13	13
Coal and coke received (tons)	256	39	18	25
Other minerals received (tons)	174	74	138	89
General goods received (tons)	237	120	104	63
Trucks of livestock handled	62	79	70	58

65.　　Looking south in the same year, we note the Army waiting room and toilets on the right. The canopy is on the booking office, which was staffed until 6th May 1968. Most of the crossing cottage is obscured. Both facilities for gentlemen are devoid of a roof. They could be very busy when troop trains were present. There had once been a 5-lever signal box; its rodding tunnel is evident on the platform face. (C.L.Caddy)

LLANGELYNIN

66.   The halt was opened on 7th July 1930 and is shown at the top of the last map. The platform was on the east side of the line and is seen in 1964. The term "Halt" was dropped in 1968. (C.L.Caddy)

67.   The 13.15 class 101 Pwllheli to Machynlleth was recorded on 2nd October 1971. Closure came on 28th October 1991, as a result of a demand for lighting by the HSE. The shelter had blown into a field in 1990. (C.L.Caddy)

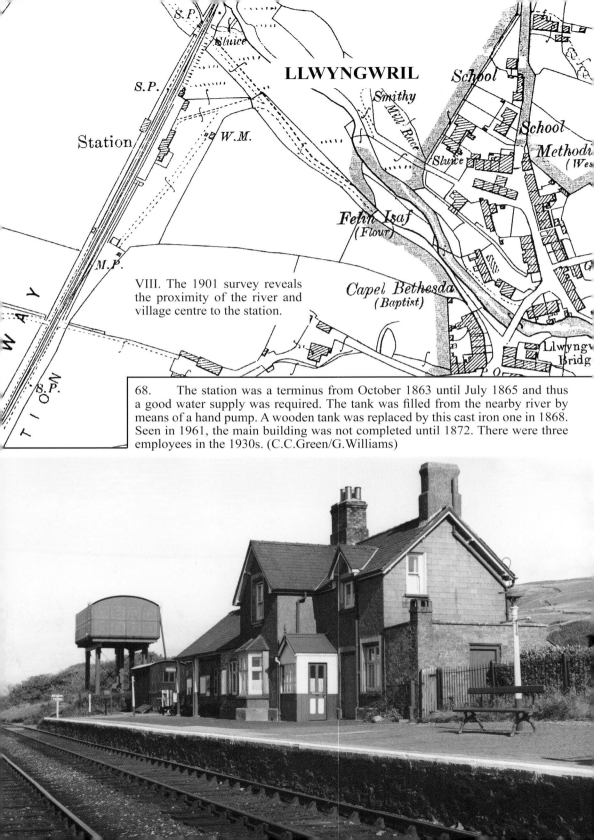

LLWYNGWRIL

Station

VIII. The 1901 survey reveals the proximity of the river and village centre to the station.

Capel Bethesda (Baptist)

Felin Isaf (Flour)

68.   The station was a terminus from October 1863 until July 1865 and thus a good water supply was required. The tank was filled from the nearby river by means of a hand pump. A wooden tank was replaced by this cast iron one in 1868. Seen in 1961, the main building was not completed until 1872. There were three employees in the 1930s. (C.C.Green/G.Williams)

69.   A common belief is that GWR stands for "God's Wonderful Railway". Long dismissed is "Great Way Round", but here is an alternative proposition from the company's own journal. (GWR Magazine)

70.   The original water supply continued to be used to the end of steam, as witnessed in about 1963. No. 82003 was one of the popular Standard class 2 2-6-2Ts. (J.W.T.House/C.L.Caddy coll.)

71.   The 10.45 Pwllheli to Machynlleth calls on 2nd May 1968, by which time the water column was redundant. There are steps by the column, instead of a ramp. The down platform had been lengthened in 1909 for Territorial Army traffic. (R.F.Roberts/SLS coll.)

72.   The date is 29th June 1969 and staffing would cease at the end of the year. The goods shed is on the left and a camping coach is in the distance. (C.L.Caddy)

73.   The signal box had a 13-lever frame and was in use from 16th March 1891 until 5th November 1972. It is seen on 23rd May 1972 as no. 5074 waits for a discussion to end. (C.L.Caddy)

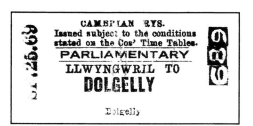

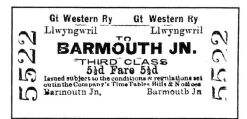

74.   The 15.56 from Pwllheli runs towards the end of the long loop on 5th October 1972. Only the up line would be used in subsequent years and the platform would take only two cars. The goods yard had closed on 4th May 1965; there had earlier been a cattle pen on the left. (C.L.Caddy)

Llwyngwril	1923	1929	1930	1933
Passenger tickets issued	16494	17039	16680	17739
Season tickets issued	70	38	46	99
Parcels forwarded	2657	3355	3400	3603
General goods forwarded (tons)	26	48	28	41
Coal and coke received (tons)	316	258	325	182
Other minerals received (tons)	1334	751	880	295
General goods received (tons)	471	597	386	338
Trucks of livestock handled	73	89	100	70

75.   Having to construct the railway on a 9ft wide ledge 100ft above Friog Rocks was difficult enough, without having a public highway above it and a belligerent mine owner wanting to extend tunnels under it for lead, copper and gold. The latter problem went away, but the former only became wider. The first major accident was on 1st January 1883, when part of the road and its wall fell on the track in the dark and derailed 2-4-0 no. 29 *Pegasus* and its train. The crew died. The bridge for miners is evident, as is one of the adit entrances. These were later lined with brick in place of wooden props. Defence work continues intermittently. (A.Dudman coll.)

76.   The second disaster was on 4th March 1933 when ex-CR 0-6-0 no. 54 (GWR no. 874) ran into rocks displaced by a heavy lorry. The loco fell to the beach, but the four coaches remained on the track. Again the crew died. This avalanche shelter was then constructed, using extensive rock bolting. It acts as a deflector and also gives structural support to the repositioned highway. It is seen from a "Dukedog" travelling south in about 1955. (M.Whitehouse coll.)

← 77. The A493 is top right and Fairbourne is in the distance, with Barmouth Bridge beyond. The 12.10 Pwllheli to Dovey Junction is climbing the 1 in 55 gradient on 24th June 1981. The descent at 1 in 66 starts in the shelter. (T.Heavyside)

78. Again Barmouth is in the background, but much less developed. Climbing towards the shelter is an ex-CR 0-6-0, but no details were recorded. This panorama is now adorned by a rare line of World War II tank traps. (P.Q.Treloar coll.)

Gt Western Ry   Gt Western Ry
Fairbourne   Fairbourne
BARMOUTH JN.
THIRD CLAS
1½d Fare 1½d
Issued subject to the conditions&regu'ations set out in the Company'sTimeTables,Bills&Notices
BarmouthJn   BarmouthJn
5293

CAMBRIAN RAILWAYS.
Issued subject to the Conditions stated in the Companys Time Tables
FAIRBOURNE   To
LLWYNGWRIL
THIRD CLASS PARLY   FARE ·/2½
Fairbourne   Fairbourne
Llwyngwril   Llwyngwril

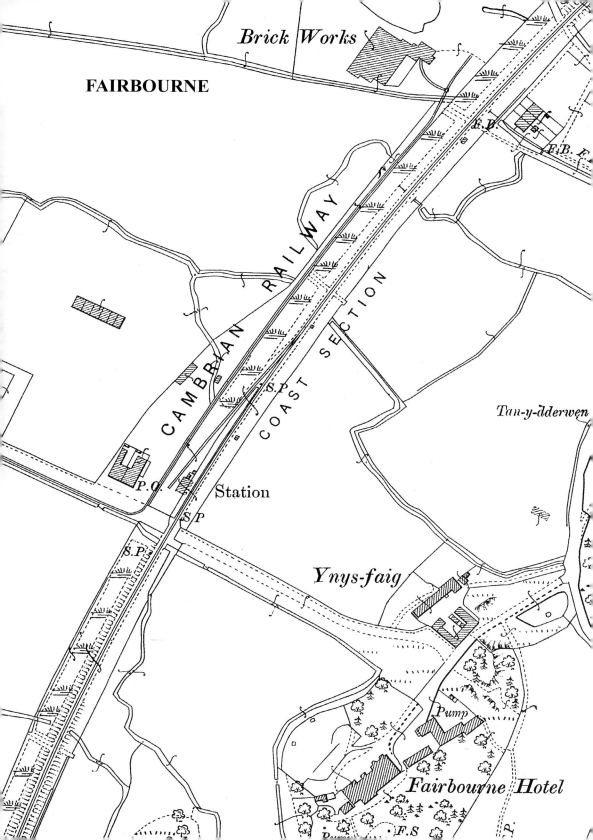

IX.　　Barmouth Ferry station was here from 3rd July 1865 until 3rd June 1867, when Barmouth Bridge opened. It was also known as Morfa Henddol. Ynys-faig Siding was on the site from 1869 to about 1890 and served a quarry. The present station opened on 1st July 1897 and is seen on the map of 1901. The tramway from the brickworks was a horse-drawn two-foot gauge line, used mainly for the conveyance of building materials for housing estates being created by Mr. McDougall, who had made his fortune by developing self-raising flour.

79.　　A train to Pwllheli runs past a CR signal and over the level crossing into the station on 5th August 1953. No. 9002 is a 4-4-0 of the "Dukedog" class. (H.F.Wheeller/ R.S.Carpenter coll.)

Fairbourne	1923	1929	1930	1933
Passenger tickets issued	21342	21356	21182	20032
Season tickets issued	47	38	50	55
Parcels forwarded	4126	4226	4113	3906
General goods forwarded (tons)	57	58	54	25
Coal and coke received (tons)	349	243	132	84
Other minerals received (tons)	303	411	348	188
General goods received (tons)	281	402	348	261
Trucks of livestock handled	17	8	5	10

80.   The goods shed is on the left as 0-6-0 no. 2255 runs in from the north in the 1950s. There were two men in the 1930s, but staffing ceased on 6th May 1968. (A.J.B.Dodd/P.Chancellor coll.)

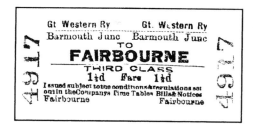

81.   A 1962 panorama has the eight-lever signal box in the centre. It closed that year, having opened in 1891. The lamp hut is on the right. The platform will take four coaches. (P.J.Garland/R.S.Carpenter coll.)

82.   The goods siding closed on 4th May 1964, the month in which the camping coach was photographed on it. A small lever frame had been installed near the gates, in place of the signal box. (C.L.Caddy)

FAIRBOURNE RAILWAY

The Terminus

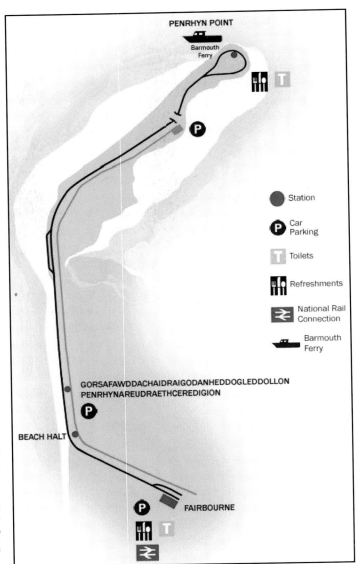

X.   The railway was 15ins gauge from 1916 until 1985. The 2004 route diagram is little altered from the original, except that the loop at the northern end did not exist prior to 1986; neither did the tunnel. The inland part of the route was provided with a third rail in 1926 to create an 18ins gauge section for a 4-2-2 model built in 1898, but it was not a success here. (Fairbourne Railway)

83.   The 2ft gauge tramway marked on map IX was carrying passengers by 1900 and continued to do so until 1916, when it was relaid to 15ins gauge. A miniature 4-4-2 named *Prince Edward of Wales* was provided by Bassett Lowke. The Eaton Hall Railway's 0-4-0T *Katie* arrived indirectly in 1924 and the 4-4-2 *Count Louis* was built for the line in 1925. (Fairbourne Railway)

84.　The railway was closed during World War II. *Count Louis* is seen on 5th August 1953; it had been completed for Count Louis Zbrowski in 1924. In the background is a CR signal and the Fairbourne Hotel. The station shown lasted until 1962. (H.F.Wheeller/R.S.Carpenter coll.)

XI.　The first building was on the site of the gift shop and the second is shown as a workshop on this 2009 plan. This extended layout was created from 1985 onwards by decking over the stream shown on map IX. (Fairbourne Railway)

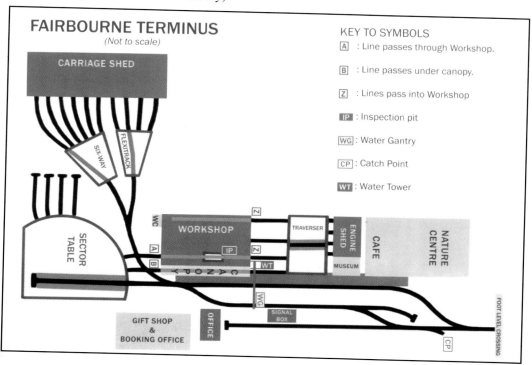

FAIRBOURNE TERMINUS
(Not to scale)

CARRIAGE SHED

SIX-WAY

FLEXITRACK

SECTOR TABLE

WC

WORKSHOP

IP

Z

Z

TRAVERSER

ENGINE SHED

MUSEUM

WT

CAFE

NATURE CENTRE

A

B

Y P O N A C

WG

GIFT SHOP & BOOKING OFFICE

OFFICE

SIGNAL BOX

CP

FOOT LEVEL CROSSING

KEY TO SYMBOLS

A　: Line passes through Workshop.

B　: Line passes under canopy.

Z　: Lines pass into Workshop

IP : Inspection pit

WG : Water Gantry

CP : Catch Point

WT : Water Tower

85.   The new station was recorded on 14th September 1978 with *Siân* waiting to leave. The locomotive was built in 1963 by G&S Light Engineering of Stourbridge. This firm also produced three other locomotives for the line. On the right is *Sylvia* which was built in 1961. (T.Heavyside)

86.   The railway changed hands again at the beginning of 1984 and at the end of the next year the gauge was reduced to 12¼ins. New track was laid and equipment was brought from France. Built to this gauge in 1978 by David Curwen, *Yeo* was first named *Jubilee*. The 2-6-2T was modelled on a Lynton & Barnstaple Railway engine and was photographed on 2nd August 1991. (M.J.Stretton)

Steam locomotives 2009

No.	Name	Builder	Type	Year
1	*Yeo*	Curwen	2-6-2T	1978
2	*Beddgelert*	Curwen	0-6-4ST	1979
4	*Sherpa*	Milner	0-4-0ST	1978
5	*Russell*	Milner	2-6-4T	1985

G. W. R.
BARMOUTH BRIDGE PROMENADE.
WEEKLY TICK
Available to date.
Charge 6d.
Contractor of Tolls—G. VERNON PRICE.

87.   *Count Louis* stops at Bathing Beach Halt, as it was called in the late 1950s. The crowds would soon move to Mediterranean beaches and the locomotive was eventually preserved by the Little Giant Trust. (M.Whitehouse coll.)

88.   *Siân* is turning from west to north on 14th September 1978. The gable end of the terminus is at the far end of the road. Note that there was a high proportion of covered coaches by that time. (T.Heavyside)

89.   *Count Louis* is returning to Fairbourne on 21st August 1952 and is at the loop, while the petrol engined 0-4-4-0 locomotive *Dingo* arrives. It was built by Wilkins & Mitchell in 1951 and dismantled in 1974. (H.F.Wheeller/R.S.Carpenter coll.)

90.   *Siân* was recorded soon after leaving the Ferry on 14th September 1978. Wind-blown sand is not kind to locomotive running gear. Fairbourne is in the background. (T.Heavyside)

The Ferry

91. *Count Louis* waits at the north end of the route on 21st August 1953, with the Mawddach Estuary and Barmouth in the background. (H.F.Wheeller/R.S.Carpenter)

92. The refreshment coach was photographed at the end of the line on the same day. The wagon contained batteries and the ventilators released the hydrogen. (H.F.Wheeller/R.S.Carpenter)

93.   Vastly improved refreshment facilities were available in the Pavilion from 1986. *Yeo* has just arrived. The line to the left had not been used regularly since 2004, owing to movement of the sand dunes over it. The locomotive has used the loop behind the train. The date of the photograph is August 2004. The line in the foreground is a siding. (Fairbourne Railway)

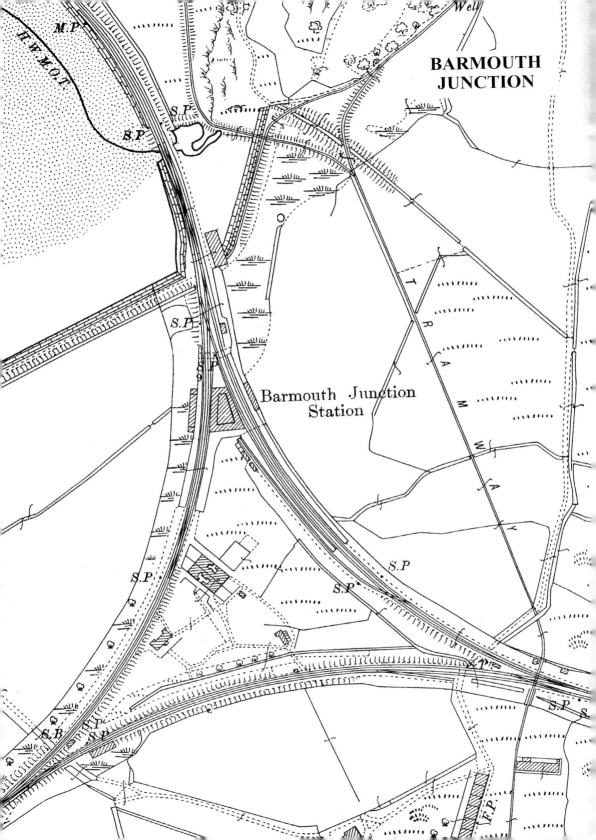

**BARMOUTH
JUNCTION**

Well

M.P.

S.P.

S.P.

S.P.

S.P.

Barmouth Junction
Station

T R A M W A Y

S.P.

S.P.

S.P.

S.P.

S.B.

S.P.

S.P.

S.P.S.

F.P.

← XII. The 1901 map has our route lower left and the approach to Barmouth Bridge at the top. At this time there was no path to the station. The line to Dolgelley is the top one on the right, the lower one being a long siding. The track across the bottom had a timber platform earlier, but only the path to it is shown. Branching from it is Andrews' Siding; the tramways shown also belonged to him. Solomon Andrews was a major property developer and tramway owner in both Cardiff and Pwllheli, his trams from the latter running to Llanbedrog. The tramway shown mainly conveyed stone from his quarry beyond the main road to the south, northwards to a site on the shore of the Mawddach, where he constructed a row of luxury dwellings with splendid vistas: Jubilee Terrace stands today. His wagons crossed four CR tracks on a transporter wagon with flangless wheels.

94.   Andrews started work here in 1896 and this is St. Mary's Terrace "for the lower orders", plus a section of his 3ft gauge tramway, from a stone quarry. In 1902, he built this road to the station as part of an agreement with CR connected with the development of his Barmouth Junction Estate. The passenger trams had limited use and were returned to his other tramways. All work had ceased by 1906 and the scheme was a failure, but most of the embankments remain as a memorial to it. This is a northward view from beyond the bottom of the map. His shed north of the station included a refreshment room and was where the passenger trams started. Two tramcars were delivered in August 1899. (Andrews Archive)

95.   No. 75 stands with a Dolgelley to Barmouth freight train in about 1918. The locomotive was built by Neilson for the CR in 1894 and became GWR no. 878. There were nine employees in 1923, but this was reduced to six in 1932. (H.W.Burman/G.Williams coll.)

96.   This array of CR signals is seen from the south end of Barmouth Bridge in 1933. In the distance is the station and the bushes on the left are close to one of the embankments of Andrews' tramway. (R.S.Carpenter coll.)

Gt. Western Ry   Gt. Western Ry
BarmouthJn   BarmouthJn
8086   TO   9808
ARTHOG
THIRD   CLASS
2d C Fare 2d C
Arthog   Arthog
FOR CONDITIONS SEE BACK W.H

97.   Moving closer to the station, we see the ends of two up trains from the footpath which passes over Barmouth Bridge. It is September 1940. Passengers cross the tracks on the level. (J.W.Sparrowe/R.S.Carpenter coll.)

MORFA MAWDDACH

98.   The name was changed from Barmouth Junction on 13th June 1960 and the junction was photographed on 22nd March 1962. On the left is 2-6-0 no. 78005 with a Dovey Junction to Barmouth train; centre is 0-6-0 no. 2286 with a train in the reverse direction and on the right is 4-6-0 no. 7821 *Ditcheat Manor* with a Ruabon to Barmouth service. (M.A.N.Johnston)

99.　　On the right is the Dolgelley bay platform. This was used for a camp coach from May 1934 and probably until the war. There was a staff of six for most of the 1930s and up to nine earlier. Goods traffic ceased on 4th November 1963; this photograph was taken a few months previously. (P.J.Garland/R.S.Carpenter coll.)

100.　　No. 75002 rumbles over the pointwork on 15th June 1964 with a Pwllheli to Shrewsbury express. Barmouth is in the left background. There had been three signal boxes from 1892 to 1913. (C.C.Green/G.Williams coll.)

101.   A view in the other direction on 12th July 1964 features the Sundays-only 9.00am
Machynlleth to Barmouth, hauled by 2-6-2T no. 82021. The 1931 signal box had 38 levers and
was in use until 15th June 1968. (C.L.Caddy)

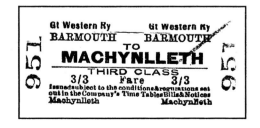

102.   The north elevation of the fondly remembered station can be compared with the other end which is shown in picture no. 99. A gasworks had been planned here, but the ground proved too unstable. Staffing ceased on 6th May 1968. The centre door had served a refreshment room for many years. (Lens of Sutton coll.)

103.   The Dolgelley line platforms were still intact at the end of 1970, but the building was about to be demolished. On the left is the lamp hut; although the station had for long been electrically lit, the signals were not. (R.Ruffell/M.J.Stretton coll.)

104.   The 10.42 Shrewsbury to Pwllheli was recorded on 24th June 1981, with a class 108 leading. Even the timber crossing had been removed and closure was expected. (T.Heavyside)

105.   The platform level was raised greatly in 1986 and the length provided was for four coaches. A waterfront footpath from here almost to Dolgellau can now be enjoyed, it being on the former trackbed. (C.L.Caddy)

106.   The eight-span iron section was fitted with a drawbridge, but in 1899 these parts were all replaced with steel components and a swingbridge, as seen in the following photographs. All trains were horse-drawn from the opening on 3rd June 1867 until October of that year. (C.C.Green coll.)

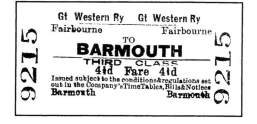

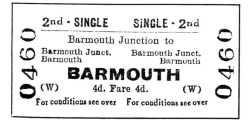

107.   The bridge is 800yds in length and has 500 piers. The swinging span is 113ft in length. This 1920s postcard includes the commencement of the footpath over the bridge and the shed for the lifeboat (left), which is launched under the track. (P.Q.Treloar coll.)

108.   No. 54 was originally named Palmerston. The 2-4-0 was built by Sharp Stewart in 1865 and lasted until 1909. Near the gate is the toll hut for pedestrians and on the left is Barmouth Tunnel. (P.Q.Treloar coll.)

109.   A rare opening was recorded on 18th September 1977 and less than three years later, one of the 113 timber piers was found to have moved, due to the activities of shipworms. All locomotives were banned immediately and a severe speed restriction enforced. Service over the bridge ceased from 12th October 1980 until 22nd May 1981 for temporary repairs. Major work followed and locomotives were allowed again from 13th April 1986. (C.L.Caddy)

110.   A few steam-hauled trips were run in August 1987 and 4-6-0 no. 7819 *Hinton Manor* creeps round the curve on the 2nd with the "Cardigan Bay Express". Arriva Trains Wales operated steam in the Summer of 2005 and it appeared in subsequent Summers, thanks to West Coast Railways. A major upgrade of the bridge was completed in 2003. (H.Ballantyne)

111.   Barmouth Tunnel is 70yds in length and its south portal is seen in June 1961. Few such structures have a cutting above, but this one was for the main road. The end of the bridge footpath is included. (R.S.Carpenter)

112.   After passing through Barmouth Tunnel, sometime in 1961, no. 2204 would soon run over Old Chapel Viaduct (78yds), which had 12 timber spans on wooden piles until rebuilt in 1952 in concrete. (P.Q.Treloar coll.)

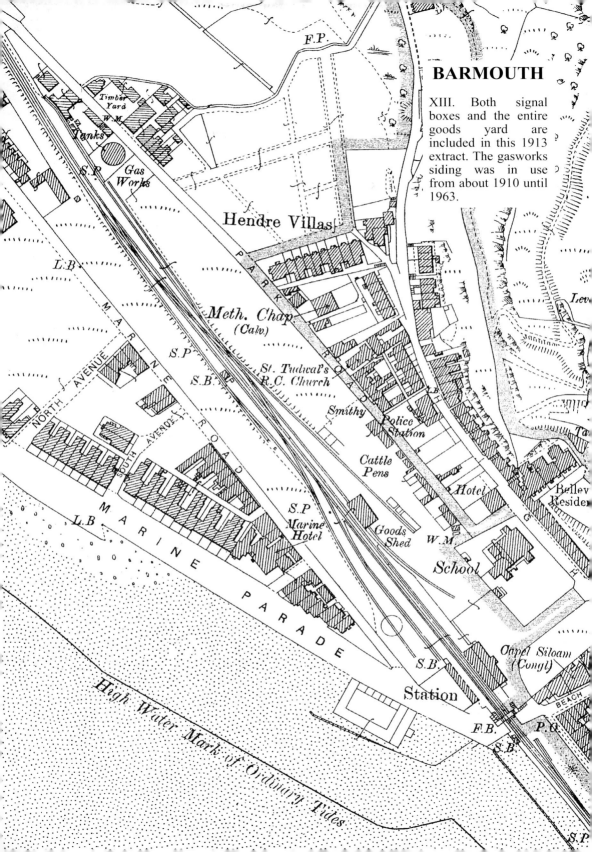

F.P.

BARMOUTH

XIII. Both signal boxes and the entire goods yard are included in this 1913 extract. The gasworks siding was in use from about 1910 until 1963.

Timber Yard
W.M.

Tanks

S.P.

Gas Works

Hendre Villas

L.B.

Meth. Chap.
(Calv)

St. Tudwal's
R.C. Church

S.P.

S.B.

Smithy

Police Station

Cattle Pens

Hotel

Bellev Reside

S.P.
Marine Hotel

Goods Shed

W.M.

School

L.B.

Lev

Ta

S.B.

Capel Siloam
(Congl)

BEACH

High Water Mark of Ordinary Tides

Station

F.B.

S.B.

P.O.

S.P.

113.   The GWR added this bay platform south of the level crossing in about 1924. The train of six-wheelers is headed by 4-4-0 no. 1091, a Sharp Stewart creation for the CR in 1893. The train is probably bound for Machynlleth. (R.M.Casserley coll.)

114.   The up bay is seen again as the 8.15am Machynlleth to Pwllheli approaches on 9th August 1948. The autocoach will be hauled to Dolgelley by 0-4-2T no. 1434. This bay was used for that service regularly. There were 17 to 21 employees in 1923-38. (W.A.Camwell/SLS coll.)

➔ 115.   The goods shed and carriage sidings are included in this view of Barbara Mitchell's headboard on the Paddington to Minffordd special on 30th April 1957. The locomotive is 4-6-0 no. 7817 *Garsington Manor* and it had taken over the train from *City of Truro* at Ruabon, which had run from Wolverhampton. (N.F.Gurley/P.Johnson coll.)

➔   116.   Approaching South Box in July 1957 is 4-4-0 "Dukedog" no. 9017, subsequently preserved on the Bluebell Railway. The double track becomes single in the distance. Note the severe temporary speed restriction. South Box had a 27-lever frame. (J.W.T.House/C.L.Caddy coll.)

117.   Brighton-built 2-6-4T no. 80080 accelerates the 2.20pm to Dovey Junction on 17th October 1964. No. 46508 waits in the bay to work the 2.55 to Chester. (L.W.Rowe)

118. The up bay was little used after the end of steam. It is seen on 28th June 1969, as the 17.07 Pwllheli to Machynlleth departs, formed of class 103 DMUs. The signal box was moved to the Llangollen Railway in 1998. It had closed on 22nd October 1988. (C.L.Caddy)

Barmouth Junction	1923	1929	1930	1933
Passenger tickets issued	15353	13825	14491	13691
Season tickets issued	24	27	25	45
Parcels forwarded	867	733	716	744
General goods forwarded (tons)	48	19	24	29
Coal and coke received (tons)	10	8	7	9
Other minerals received (tons)	377	66	29	10
General goods received (tons)	142	51	43	51
Trucks of livestock handled	57	64	46	38

Other views of this station can be found in
Barmouth to Pwllheli.

119.   Two views from 1st September 2008 reveal the station to be in good order and still with a passing loop, albeit controlled from Machynlleth. Tickets could still be purchased, not from a conventional booking office, but from a well stocked and helpful Tourist Information Centre. (V.Mitchell)

120.   Both platforms retained good weather protection, the up side keeping its cast iron stanchions. The 09.36 class 158 from Pwllheli was the fourth of ten trains available from Barmouth to Machynlleth that day, a vastly improved service. (V.Mitchell)

MP Middleton Press
EVOLVING THE ULTIMATE RAIL ENCYCLOPEDIA

Easebourne Lane, Midhurst, West Sussex.
GU29 9AZ Tel:01730 813169
www.middletonpress.co.uk email:info@middletonpress.co.uk
A-978 0 906520 B- 978 1 873793 C- 978 1 901706 D-978 1 904474 E - 978 1 906008

OOP Out of print at time of printing - Please check availability   BROCHURE AVAILABLE SHOWING NEW TITLES